IMAGES OF ENGLAND

FORMBY
FRESHFIELD
AND ALTCAR

A ploughing team at work on Kirklake Bank, on land between Wicks Lane and Kirklake Road. The land was poor, so rye was grown. This had a long stalk which was excellent for thatching. These fields are now covered by St Jerome's church, schools and houses.

IMAGES OF ENGLAND

FORMBY
FRESHFIELD
AND ALTCAR

BARBARA AND REGINALD YORKE

TEMPUS

Crowds gather at Formby Council Offices in Freshfield Road to hear the Chairman of Formby Urban District Council, Peggy Beeston, make the Official Proclamation of Queen Elizabeth II's accession on 8 February 1952. This imposing building had been formally opened in 1927, replacing the previous Council Offices in Church Road. The land and building cost £6,200. It remained the hub of municipal life in Formby, its council chamber being fully used for council meetings, courts, civic affairs and voluntary organizations, until local government re-organization led to the creation of Merseyside County Council and Sefton MBC in 1974.

First published 2000, reprinted 1999, 2006

Tempus Publishing Limited
The Mill, Brimscombe Port,
Stroud, Gloucestershire, GL5 2QG

British Library Cataloguing in Publication Data.
A catalogue record for this book is available from the British Library.

ISBN 0 7524 1181 0

Typesetting and origination by Tempus Publishing Limited
Printed in Great Britain

Contents

Acknowledgements

We are extremely glad to have had this opportunity to share our ongoing interest in the history of Formby and its surrounding area with others. We are even more grateful to all those who have directly or indirectly helped with the provision of photographs, illustrations and information. We must also thank our many interested friends for their helpful anecdotes and advice.

First and foremost, we must thank the Formby Society whose rich archives we have, with permission, raided. We have expressed our debt to its founder members in the Introduction. We have tried to support the pictures with accurate, if brief, historical information where available and have listed some of our main sources. If we have made mistakes, please let us know!

The collection and processing of all this material would not have been possible without the personal back-up, support and help of members of our immediate family, in particular Rebecca and Jack Melling and Nigel and Rebecca Yorke. Finally we are grateful to our local librarians, professional colleagues and friendly local bookshop.

Photograph credits:
The Formby Society, Dr R.K. Gresswell, *The Formby Times*, Clayton Reynolds, Muriel Sibley, Formby High School, Mrs Sawyer, George Grant, Lillian Rushton, Mrs Tyrer, Edith Kelly, Phil and Muriel Clulee, Mr Needham, Aldon Ferguson, National Railway Museum, Arthur Sutton, John Chapman, Formby UDC, John Wyles, Mrs Jean Noble, John Houston (Sefton Coastal Management), Cath Williams NMGM, Dr Richard Sloan, John Rathbone, Harry and Gladys Bevan, Bob Wagstaff, Austen Cartmel, Michael Cook, Tom Moss, Gordon Roberts, Mike Gee (English Nature), Mrs Ted Turner, James McGregor, Mrs Phyllis Owen, Mike Dean (Historical Radar Archive), Alec Watson, Mrs J. Castle, John Hughes.

Main historical sources:
Victoria County History: Lancashire; *Formby Reminiscences* by C. Jacson; *Viking Village* ed. Edith Kelly; *Formby and Freshfield in Times Past* by Barbara Yorke; *Britain's First Lifeboat Station* by B. and R. Yorke.

Other sources:
Unfortunately space does not permit a full listing of the other local history documents and publications we have referred to. Should anyone need this we can provide the full list of references used.

Introduction

This book is largely a panoramic series of snapshots of Formby's past. For very many years local residents have been interested in the history of their village. This interest goes back as far as the Revd Robert Cort, the Curate of St Peter's, who died in 1852. He recounted visiting an old man on his death-bed in 1787, the last inhabitant of the original village which was overwhelmed by sand dunes. This old man, who lived in a 'low house on the verge of the old burying ground', declared that as a boy he remembered an 'old harbour' and 'jumping from ship to ship'.

Another widely believed local legend is that the first potatoes grown in England were taken from a wrecked vessel and planted in the neighbourhood of Formby. In a similar fashion the Revd Cort recounted how in 1736 a ship laden with tobacco was wrecked and 'for fifty years afterwards every man, woman and child that came to speak to him in the Vestry was smoking'. Certainly in the earlier centuries the 'sand grounders' led peculiarly isolated lives, depending on the sea for food and fuel; the Moss supplied peat and fish. A great deal of our history, as Professor Kelly remarked, is 'much older than we think'.

Since the emergence of photography we have been able to record the appearances of old buildings, the people and their occupations in a way impossible in the past. We are also grateful for the rich written record which backs this up and explains it all. Much of this material was collected by the Formby Society after it was formed in the early 1950s and has been steadily added to since. It has been particularly enriched by the efforts of early members of the society who followed a tradition started by the Formby family of keeping scrapbooks of newspaper cuttings and collecting and indexing old photographs. Two early members of the society, Fred Beardswood and William Marshallsey, independently compiled some *Notes on the History of Formby*.

Muriel Sibley, having arrived here in the late 1940s, 'fell in love with the place', and spent the rest of her life photographing, drawing and painting the vanishing world of thatched cottages and leafy lanes. The Sibley Collection, now cared for by the Formby Society, is a unique archive in its own right. Her friend, Miss Lillian Rushton, just before her death in 1982, worked a beautiful Formby equivalent of the Bayeux Tapestry, a large embroidery recording some highlights of our history.

The first definitive account of the history of Formby, *Viking Village*, was written and edited by Edith Kelly and originally published by the Formby Society in 1973, but for many years has been out of print. The present book follows the success of *Formby and Freshfield in Times Past*, written in 1982, which has also long been unavailable. Nevertheless there is a strong and continuing interest in our township and its environs and local history is now part of the school syllabus and often the subject of academic research and dissertations. This interest has been increased further by the approach of the new millennium. It is truly an appropriate time to review our recorded past, which here in Formby goes back to the Domesday Book.

In this panoramic view of our heritage we have had to skate over the surface fairly superficially but hope we will lead others to look through the windows we have opened and then be tempted to explore them more fully.

Barbara and Reg Yorke, 1999

'The gas man cometh.' The first gas lighting in Formby was in Chapel Lane, using acetylene gas, at the turn of the century (see p. 9). The Formby Gas Company was established in 1877 with a gasworks and gasometer in Watchyard Lane at Smithy Green. This was taken over by the Liverpool Gas Company in 1934. Local production of gas ceased in the 1950s and finally town gas was replaced by natural gas from the national supply in the early 1970s. This fitter is burning off the last of the town gas.

One

Formby: The Heart of the Village

'The Heart of the Village' as it appeared from the corner of Three Tuns Lane in around 1900. The picture was taken by S.B. Reynolds, a local photographer who subsequently emigrated to Canada. The street lamp on the left was Formby's first experiment with street lighting, using acetylene gas. The policeman is Inspector Fyfe and Mr Birtwistle the grocer is wearing the white coat. Also visible is Mr Hayworth, a draper.

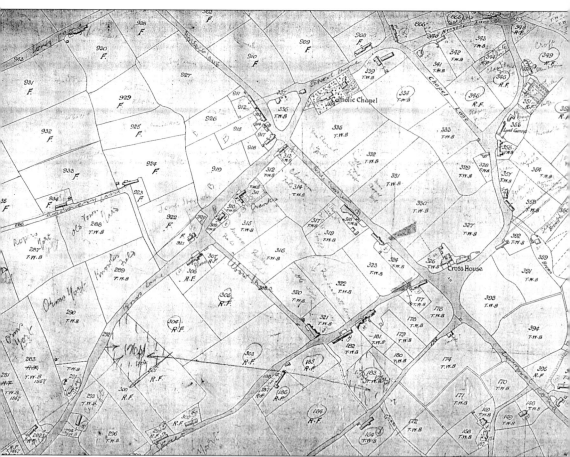

Detail from a tithe map, 1845. The main road through the village was originally called Brows Lane throughout its length. Together with School Lane, this can in many ways be considered the heart of the village as it is known today. Its dramatic development in the second half of the nineteenth century, following the arrival of the railway, heralded the expansion of Formby and Freshfield which has continued ever since. The only buildings present in 1845 were seven cottages, four on one side and three on the other, separated by spacious gardens, arable land and meadow. One of these cottages, near the corner with Elbow Lane, was occupied by Dr Richard Sumner, the village doctor, an important figure in the village and famous for his heroism in assisting a famous lifeboat rescue. His memory is now commemorated by the name of a local road. There were only fourteen other inhabitants in the heart of the village (Brows Lane/School Lane) in 1851: the parish priest, the doctor's family (which included two sisters-in-law, running a small private school), a lady 'landed proprietor', five farmers, a cow-keeper and four agricultural labourers, one retired. The farmers between them farmed just 64 acres. By 1900 (see opposite), the scene had changed dramatically. On the south side, all the cottages except one had gone, replaced by a more or less continuous row of houses and shops and two banks. Some shops on the north side were provided with fashionable covered verandas and one became the Post Office.

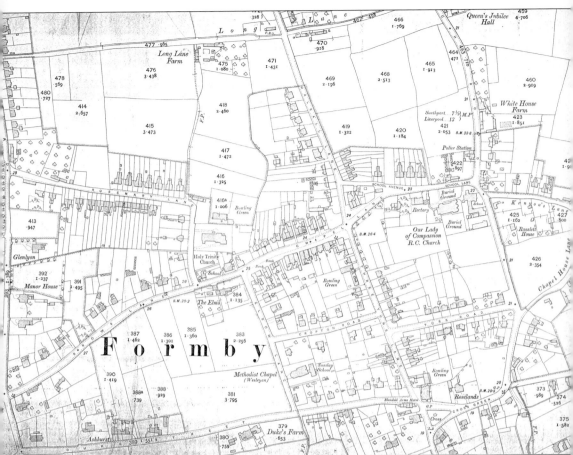

The same area in 1907, in a detail from an Ordnance Survey map. By 1900, Holy Trinity School had appeared at the western end of the village, with Holy Trinity church and church hall situated behind it, facing Rosemary Lane. Due to the increase in population, the Church of England parish had been split into three. The remaining cottage opposite the school had become known as the Elms and would later become the Priory, a prominent feature of the village until it was demolished to make way for shops in the 1960s. School Lane was the site of the original village school (which still survives as a restaurant). The old Catholic chapel was sited opposite, with a house and burial ground, but was later superseded by Our Lady's Roman Catholic church. On the corner with Church Road a further cottage, fold and garden occupied the site of the subsequent Catholic school, now the site of retirement flats. By 1900 the influx of new occupants following the arrival of the railway had produced an entirely new population mix. This still included the parish priest but by now there was only one farmer; there were several market gardeners and miscellaneous other workers, such as coal agents, coal carter, dressmaker, joiner, financial agent, book-keeper, porter, postmaster, erector of iron buildings, newsagent, chemist, accountant, printer, wool dealer, general manager, monthly nurse, general draper, poulterer, confectioner, house painter and master butcher. This last was William Charters, the founder of the family business which survived in the same place until 1998. By 1925 that part of Brows Lane east of Rosemary Lane had been renamed Chapel Lane.

T.N. Slater, 'grocers and provision, wine and spirit merchant'. Built on the corner with Halsall Lane, started by Thomas Slater and later run by his two sons Neville and Wilf, it closed in 1950 and passed to new owners. Together with the other shops in the same block it was demolished in 1990. The next shop became the Lancashire County Library from 1939 to 1961. From the 1950s it was run very efficiently by Mrs S.E. Derbyshire, until the new library in Duke Street was opened. Next to the library (which became a barber's, a book-maker's and for a time the office of *The Formby Times*), was Mr Needham, an electrician who retired when the building was demolished, leaving his farewell message on the empty window: 'Goodbye Formby'.

The 'Homesteader'. Mr. Nimmo was an enterprising and excellent joiner who bought and sold things and occasionally fixed them. He had been preceded by Samuels and Couth, builders.

The Maryland Home for the Elderly was established in 1953 largely through the endeavours of Cllr Peggy Beeston with support from the Red Cross, District Nursing Association, Personal Services Association and CVS. It provided much-needed accommodation for single elderly pensioners, there being little council accommodation provided in Formby at that time. Two adjacent houses were used, one being donated by its owner, Miss Nora Wild, and the other owned by the Urban District Council. A committee was established with Sir John Moores as its original president. The home continues its good work to this day.

Bob Howard's Cottage. Photographed from Our Lady's churchyard, this croft was occupied in 1845 by James Barton and was later tenanted by the Howard family. Bob was the village postman. His home was demolished to make room for the erection of new houses.

J. Kelly, boot-maker. Mr Kelly is taking time out of his boot-repairing to watch the photographer! This cottage and croft on the corner of Kenyons Lane was occupied by Ellis Dean, a house joiner, in 1845. He had a joinery shop and also worked an acre of arable land as a smallholding. The junction facing Our Lady's School is surprisingly narrow for what was then the main route through Formby, so it is not surprising that this cottage was demolished for road widening. The family of Ellis Dean have continued his business in Gores Lane to this day.

The Rectory. Built in 1840 next to the original chapel, the house is described in the 1855 Visitation Returns as having 'eleven rooms, in tolerable repair, having been painted in 1853, with outbuildings, including a pigsty, midden, poultry coop, coach house, stable and potting shed'. The priest at that time was Father Crowe; in 1845 Revd John Smith. The original parish included Hightown and Ainsdale.

Richard Rimmer, 'Fish, Game and Poultry Dealer, Glass and China Dealer, British and Foreign Fruiterer. Families waited on upon receipt of postcard'. This splendid shop on the corner of Three Tuns Lane was apparently photographed just before Christmas! Approximately 150 Christmas dinners are waiting to be sold and the Rimmer team look pleased with their efforts. The Rimmers were a prolific and hard-working family who continued in business until the 1960s when one of their other three shops in Chapel Lane was converted to a mini-supermarket, so starting a major trend in local retailing. According to John Tyrer, Dick Rimmer's best customer was the golf club. Rimmer's got their vegetables from Tyrer's in the twenties and thirties. Jimmy Rimmer, the head of the family in the 1940s and beyond, was very active in local government, a local magistrate, and was chairman of the Council for five periods, totalling eleven years. In the early years of the century rabbits were an important item of diet and in the 1950s were sold for a shilling each. Fines for poaching of 'conies' were commonly inflicted by the courts.

Williams & Glyn's Bank, now the Royal Bank of Scotland. In 1992 the Formby branch of Williams Deacons and Manchester and Salford Bank, (later to become Williams Deacons) celebrated 100 years of banking here. This was one of the first banks attracted by Formby's late nineteenth-century growth and prosperity, when it looked as if Formby might become a holiday resort to rival Southport. The building had originally become a bank in 1895. Williams & Glynn moved from 8 Chapel Lane in 1913. The recession in the 1920s hit Formby hard and as a consequence, the bank was taken over by the Royal Bank of Scotland in 1985. Their premises were renovated in the thirties and rebuilt in the late seventies; the building shown in the photograph was said to be 'in an extreme state of disrepair, inadequate and outdated for modern banking methods'. The bank has had only nine managers in its 100 years' history.

Charters' butchers. This was one of Formby's first butchers, in business in the same shop since before 1900, closing only in 1998. The cattle and sheep were actually slaughtered on the premises. William Charters, who was also captain of the fire brigade, celebrated the Relief of Ladysmith during the Boer War by leading a victory parade through the village on horseback. A less pleasing episode was in 1899 when there was a fire at the golf club. Captain Charters, in a one-horse trap, drove round summoning the firemen, but unfortunately the hoses were missing and when the firemen eventually arrived the club had been burnt to the ground.

The Elms. This nine-bedroom thatched farmhouse appears on the tithe map of 1845, at which date it was leased by Marjorie Knowles, a widow. One of its meadows subsequently became the football ground. Occupied from the 1920s to the 1950s by Mrs Hilda Leggate, it was renamed by a new owner, Mrs Van der Vord, who used it as a guest house and tea-room. It was badly re-thatched by a local footballer, then de-thatched and slated. It became damp and in poor condition and was demolished and replaced by a row of shops which is where the present-day post office is situated. Older residents will remember the owner's friendly green parrot.

The original post office was established at the end of the nineteenth century in an old cottage which had been occupied in 1848 by James Sherliker. This was also a general shop and was demolished in 1900 to make way for Holy Trinity School.

The second post office building, 1911. This was in bigger premises further down Chapel Lane, where Formby Travel is now situated. Here for a period the postmaster was Mr Fred Beardwood, one of Formby's earliest local historians. The shops on the north side of the village began life as private houses with front gardens, which have now been paved over.

The third post office, a splendid purpose-built shop on the corner of Rosemary Lane, erected in 1920. It had a commodious sorting office behind and telephone exchange above. This building closed as a post office in recent years but remains as a sorting and parcels office.

Midland Bank and the old cottages nearby. These cottages were the last to be occupied on the north side of Chapel Lane. Originally all the houses had front gardens like these. When converted to shops the gardens were paved over but their frontages still belong to the properties. The Midland Bank was built in the 1960s, at the time of the development of the new estates.

This shop has been a chemist's since the early years of the century. Mr Woods was the chemist here in 1891 and had a single digit telephone number. He spoke Esperanto and would dispense foreign prescriptions. He was followed by a Mr Clague and then by a man and wife team, the Bradshaws. Mrs Phyllis Bradshaw was trained in Birmingham. She became actively involved in many local organizations, including the Horticulture and Agricultural Society. The Bradshaws passed the business to Mr MacDougal, whose son still runs it.

Birtwistle's (later Dalley's) on the north side of Chapel Lane is a good example of how the houses were converted to shops. Even today the upper part of the buildings have been little altered. The veranda shelters sides of bacon hanging outside. Mr Birtwistle vied with Mr Charters by decorating his lion with coloured lights at the Relief of Ladysmith.

The back of the Chapel Lane shops, at the rear of what is now Smith's Radio and Television. At the far end was a bake-house from which bread was delivered daily by horse. Above were store rooms for flour and oats. The rooms at the top of the steps were occupied between 1945 and 1953 by a dancing school and the Formby Mounted Police kept their horses in the stable below for a period.

The Formby Society open-air art exhibition, held under the old chestnut trees, has been a regular and colourful feature of village life each June since the early 1950s. The Society was formed in 1953 with Professor Tom Kelly as president. It has remained Formby's major civic society and its only local history society. Its 500 members enjoy a wide range of activities but the open air exhibition is one of the most appealing.

This pretty cottage, seen in around 1900, was on the site of the present-day Barclays Bank. In 1848 it was occupied by a spinster, Margery Liverslie, but it was destroyed by fire in 1903. The small child in the foreground, despite appearances, is actually a boy, Clayton Reynolds. His father had a stationery and photography business in Chapel Lane. The two girls are Edith and Bella Benson together with two-year-old Lucy Reynolds. The Reynolds and Bensons subsequently emigrated to Canada.

View from the war memorial, 1954. This summer scene shows a well tended roundabout, light traffic and welcome shade in the leafy village centre. There are as yet no yellow lines. Unfortunately, the row of elms on the south side of Chapel Lane had to be removed because of Dutch elm disease in 1975. New trees were subsequently planted but will take between seventy and a hundred years to reach maturity. We expect that these trees will now out-last most of the local population!

Two

Churches

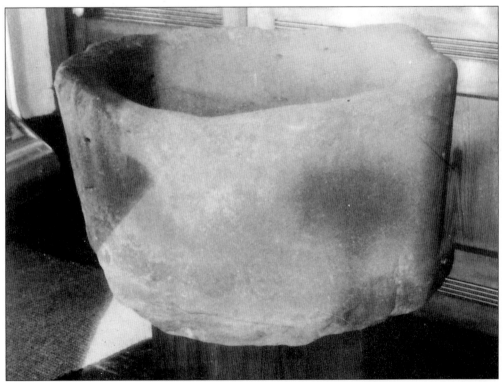

A Norman font from the earliest chapel-of-ease in the parish. For most of its early history Formby was not a parish in its own right but remained a detached portion of the parish of Walton-on-the-Hill. The chapel was probably built in the twelfth century, on the edge of the dunes, near the Kirklake in Ravenmeols. Although it was destroyed in the eighteenth century (said to have fallen a victim to the ravages of time, weather and storms), its Norman font has miraculously survived and this is Formby's oldest ancient monument.

The Godstone. The chapel was built adjacent to the original medieval settlement which is thought to have been lost under the sea and sands. Within the churchyard today may be seen the curious and mysterious Godstone of uncertain date and significance, together with the ancient village cross, removed from Cross Green in 1879, and the old village stocks which formerly stood near the green.

The Old Churchyard, a drawing by Catherine Jacson, dating from the early 1840s. She was a granddaughter of Revd Richard Formby, and was the author of *Formby Reminiscences*. The drawing shows the small but ancient graveyard among the sand dunes. After the original church had finally vanished in the eighteenth century, the graveyard remained. As it was consecrated land it continued to be used for burials.

St Luke's church. With the coming of the railway in 1848 the population began to increase and as more houses were built in the area around the station it was felt that a second Anglican church was needed. Mary Formby gave the money and her brother Dr Richard Formby gave the land for the new church. It was built adjacent to the site of the ancient chapel and opened in 1855. On the floor of the entrance porch is a memorial stone brought from York Minster, with an inscription to Richardus Fourmbi, armour bearer to Henry IV, who died in Bosworth in 1407. Percy French, poet and songwriter, is buried here.

St Peter's church. The Formby family converted to the Anglican church in 1717 and then provided several vicars to Formby. The ancient chapel in the sand dunes was 'overcome by blown sand' and became derelict in the mid-eighteenth century. In order to help pay for a new church a levy was collected throughout the country.

Renovations to St Peter's. The sundial and a bell from the old chapel were transferred to the new chapel, which was dedicated to St Peter. This was erected nearer to the new eighteenth-century centre of population, on land in Green Lane. Consecrated in 1747, it remained the only Anglican parish church in Formby for over 100 years and also served the hamlets of Ravenmeols, Ainsdale, Ince Blundell and part of Altcar.

The first Catholic chapel, in School Lane. In the 'penal' period, mass was celebrated in private houses and other buildings, including the tithe barn at Alt Grange and later the New House at Ince Blundell and Priesthouse in Formby. According to the church's centenary brochure published in 1964 'its plain exterior lends support to the idea that it was disguised as a dwelling house or barn'. It was seized during the 1688 revolution and became Formby's tithe barn for almost a century. Following this it became divided into dwellings, one of which was later occupied by the schoolmistresses Anne and Theresa Lamb. It was reclaimed for religious use in 1788 and seated 150 people. In 1930 it was converted into a convent for the Sisters of Charity of St Paul the Apostle.

The Priesthouse. The major manorial family, the Blundells, remained Catholic despite persecution. They built a house for aged Jesuits in Chapel Lane in 1701, which became the residence of the Roman Catholic priest in 1712. It housed an aumbry cupboard dating from 1691. In the tithe records of 1844 it is described as 'Chapel House'. In 1861 a subsequent tenant, Miss Sophia Earle, founded a lending library at St Peter's Girls' School. The house was taken down soon after this photograph was taken.

Our Lady's church. The new church was erected in 1864 following a rectory built in 1840, designed by the architect Henry Clutton who had previously designed several major commissions including Ruthin Castle (1853), Lille Cathedral (1875), and St Mary's, Douglas (1859), where he met Monsignor Carr, who subsequently brought him to Formby. It was provided with gas lighting in 1897 and then electric lighting in 1947, together with a new heating system. Considerable improvements followed with funds raised from August Galas and Christmas Fairs. The name of Monsignor Carr, who remained parish priest for over fifty years until the age of seventy-five, is still remembered. He was also very active in secular affairs.

Holy Trinity church. By 1890 it was felt that the population had grown to such an extent that a further Anglican church was needed. Once again land was given by a member of the Formby family, the Revd Lonsdale Formby, and after much further fundraising Holy Trinity church was built in Rosemary Lane.

Holy Trinity choir, 1897. 1 Clement Wallworth, 2 Bill Aindow, 3 Clayton Reynolds, 4 ? Dickinson, 5 Harold Beardwood, 6 Fred Aindow, 7 Bernard Makan, 8 Alec Grant, 9 P.J. Maddocks (organist), 10 Fred Kitchen, 11 John Horsefall, 12 Ernie Jenkins, 13 Percy Horsefall, 14 Jack Lowden, 15 Sidney Beardwood, 16 -?-, 17 ? Moran, 18 ? Dickinson, 19 Percy Woodfin, 20 Jack Eccles, 21 Jack Hoskin, 22 Eddie Reynolds. The information was provided by Clayton Reynolds of Toronto, Canada in 1953.

The Methodist church, Elbow Lane. Originally a Wesleyan chapel, it was built in 1874 at a cost of £637. In the entrance hall there was a vestry where members of the congregation deposited their lanterns on dark winter nights. These must have been essential when walking the unlit and unpaved lanes.

The extension to the Methodist church, 1899. With the growth of Formby in the latter part of the nineteenth century the Wesleyan Methodist congregation increased. The church was registered for marriages and baptisms, Sunday school classes were held in the schoolroom and a small day school flourished for a few years. In 1899, in the presence of a large crowd, the foundation stone for an enlarged church was laid by Mrs Edwin Cannington.

The Rose Queen at the Methodist church's Summer Garden Fête. In the 1960s and '70s the fête would start with the crowning of the Rose Queen. This crowning ceremony was preceded by a procession through the village centre. The Queen would sit in the back of an open-top car with her attendants holding ribbons attached to the car. She was usually preceded by a band. All traffic was stopped while the procession wound through the village.

In 1890 the Methodists also built a mission room at the corner of Queens Road and Sefton Road for the congregation living to the west of the railway. A simple structure of one room and a vestry, this building continued in use until the 1960s, following which it was demolished and the land used for house building.

Formby tithe barn, West Lane. At first, following the 1688 revolution, tithes were collected and stored in the chapel in School Lane. Later the tithe barn in West Lane was used, until the Commutation of the Tithes in the mid-nineteenth century, when tithes were replaced by financial payments.

St Michael's, Altcar. Altcar is one of the ancient parishes of the diocese. The earliest church stood a little to the south of the present building erected in 1879. As at Formby, an ancient font has survived. A former vicar, Revd William Warburton, described how the congregation had to reach church by boat when floods occurred, as they frequently did, in his low-lying parish. The old Church House, subsequently an inn and now Altcar Hall Farm, stands by the churchyard.

The Congregational church. Founded in 1880, the two men who instigated its establishment had originally been members of the Methodist congregation. They helped to organize the first Congregational services in the Grapes Hotel. The Congregational church flourished and a larger building was erected at a cost of £200 in 1888; the building of today was opened in 1938. This church, now known as the United Reformed church, has played a wide role in village life. In the early twentieth century ladies of the church arranged weekly afternoon meetings to enable girls in service to make friends in the community.

Three

Schools

The Old School. This school, which gave its name to the lane, was originally established in 1659. There were, however, difficulties in paying the schoolmaster and by 1688 it had been standing vacant for several years. It recommenced with funding from a new charity set up for the purpose (Marshes Charity), but the income was not sufficient to keep it going and the original building was demolished in 1785 and replaced by the present building which dates from that time. It is thus over two hundred years old. For many years used as a cottage, it is now a Grade II listed building housing a restaurant.

The original Girls' School. In 1815 a very small school for girls was conducted in an outhouse in the grounds of Formby Hall next to the dovecote, endowed by Richard Formby and with financial support from the Formby family.

St Peter's Girls' School, Paradise Lane. In 1850 Mary Formby had a new girls' school building erected in Paradise Lane, with two schoolmistresses who were paid 6s a week to teach between 95 and 100 scholars each winter (but considerably fewer in summer!). In 1858 a boys' school was built opposite with a master's house attached. These two schools are still in use as St Peter's Junior School.

St Luke's first church school. In 1855 this school was established in a small building, consisting of one large room accommodating forty pupils of all ages, on the corner of Ravenmeols Lane and King's Road. Mrs Dickinson, a schoolmistress, drove to school in a trap bringing her own two children with her. This tiny school functioned until 1911 when it was replaced by the present St Luke's Primary School in Jubilee Road, on land given by Mrs Charlotte Formby. It was occupied as a cottage until it was demolished to make way for flats.

St Luke's second school. After the building of Holy Trinity church and the change in parish boundaries, St Luke's Parish Council was very keen to build a new school in the new parish on the seaward side of the railway line. The vicar wanted to build it near the church but the Parish Council pointed out that the church was rather isolated as most houses were in the area of Andrews Lane, Jubilee Road and Queens Road. The new school built in 1911 in Jubilee Road is still in use today.

Holy Trinity School was opened opposite Elbow Lane in 1901 with 112 scholars including fifty infants, at a cost of £2,200, so relieving considerable pressure on the existing schools. Necessary fund-raising included a 'Dramatic Entertainment' at Shaftesbury House and a village fair on Poverty Field by Freshfield station. At first used for infants only, it became a school for all ages in the 1930s and an 'aided' school in 1944. The infants' department moved to a new school building in Lonsdale Road in 1962. Eventually the rest of the school also had to move. On the last day each class packed its few belongings and each pupil, carrying his own chair, walked to join the infants on Lonsdale Road.

A class of Holy Trinity School, *c.* 1905. This postcard was sent by one of the pupils to her older brother in Canada who had recently emigrated from Formby. It shows a mixed class of boys and girls who, however, had separate yards for playtimes.

Our Lady's School. A cottage existed on this site, occupied by a widow, Margaret Brown, who farmed twelve acres with the help of her two sons. Later the owner, Thomas Weld-Blundell, gave the land for a day school, which was erected in 1871 at a cost of £1,200. Further rooms were added in 1888 and in 1895 an infants' room was added. There was a further extension at the turn of the century when it was taken over by Lancashire Education Authority. Gas lighting remained until 1963 when the rising school population necessitated the start of a new school at Bull Cop. Miss Lamb was mistress of girls and infants in 1925.

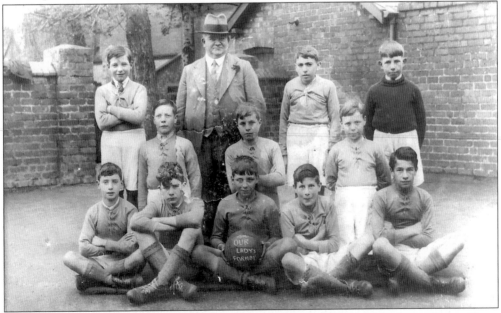

The football team of Our Lady's School in 1934, with the headmaster Mr George Ernest Ryan. This photograph was rediscovered by two boys in an empty house in Halsall Lane and given to the *Formby Times*. The local paper has published much interesting historical material since it first appeared in 1894.

The Methodist day school. In 1877 a day school was attached to the Methodist chapel but closed when Holy Trinity School opened in 1905 in Brows Lane.

The two Misses Gill and their pupils. The history of private schools in Formby is complicated, as there have been so many, mostly quite small and usually conducted in private houses. The Misses Gill ran their small girls' college in Freshfield Road, in Lendal House and in Beacon Holme.

Bishop's Court, a Roman Catholic preparatory school for boys in Wrigley's Lane. This along with Holmwood, also a boy's preparatory school with a junior department, in College Avenue, was one of a number of larger establishments. There was also St Peter's in Freshfield, which educated boys between the ages of eleven and seventeen who intended to train as priests.

St Vincent's Approved School. Formby had its share of approved schools, including St George's at Freshfield (now Clarence House), which until 1928 was a convent for girls, and St Vincent's in Ravenmeols Lane, which was originally built and run as a private mental hospital known as Shaftesbury House. It has now been demolished to make way for new housing.

Holmwood School. Opened in 1901, it occupied these purpose-built buildings in 1903. It took about 100 boys, most of them boarders, and prepared them for entrance to public schools at thirteen. It occupied extensive grounds of around ten acres so had excellent sports facilities. The school passed through many phases of expansion and in the 1980s it began to admit girls. The school closed in the late 1980s and now the area has become another housing estate with a small children's play area.

A woodwork lesson at Holmwood. An early prospectus for the school claimed that 'a good preparatory school must combine a wide variety of virtues which should influence a child for life. These virtues include self-discipline, good manners, honesty, consideration for others, together with strong moral values'. The school had an excellent academic record and a syllabus which included the arts, woodwork and games.

State education came to Formby with the establishment of a Senior Council School in 1938 on land fronting Freshfield Road at a cost of £160,000. This school was originally designed to have four classes of forty pupils each. By 1939, not surprisingly, it was outgrowing its capacity, particularly following the wartime evacuation of children from Bootle and Litherland and even as far away as Kent.

Formby High School. This school was created from the Formby County Secondary School and the former County Primary buildings and then became Formby's first comprehensive school, opened by Margaret Thatcher during her period as Minister of Education in October 1972. Up until this time, secondary education had only been provided in Waterloo, Crosby or Southport. (Photograph courtesy of Formby High School)

The Seminary, Freshfield. In 1884 a former boys' boarding school run by a Protestant clergyman was put up for sale. It was later to become a junior seminary for boys aged eleven to seventeen, who would subsequently train as priests. Originally taking some fifty boys, the house was extended twice with this large four-storey wing being added in 1928 to house 120 scholars. Due to changing needs it was closed in 1972. The buildings were then taken over by the Leonard Cheshire Foundation but were not entirely suitable and so were demolished and replaced by the splendid purpose-built buildings of today. The grounds contain the graves of some Mill Hill missionaries.

Local children with their teachers, Mr and Mrs Scott, at St Michael's, Altcar, in March 1923. The school was behind a house built for the teacher dated 1865. This still stands, opposite the end of Engine Lane. This school closed in 1929 and pupils then had the choice of going to school in Haskayne or Formby. An earlier school still stands further on the road to Hillhouse with a date stone of 1821.

Four

Lanes and Cottages

Greenwood's map of Formby, 1818. This map, the earliest of any accuracy, shows that the old village, near the dunes, had by then been deserted. There are now two centres of population, one around the Old Mill, the other around the southern boundary. The Town Fields are the uninhabited, unenclosed area to the West of Downholland Brook on the reclaimed Formby Moss. Altcar Road had not yet been constructed. The roads out of Formby to the East are North Moss Lane, Downholland Moss Lane and via the Fleam Bridge to the village of Great Altcar. St Peter's church does not appear, but the old Catholic chapel is shown in its present position.

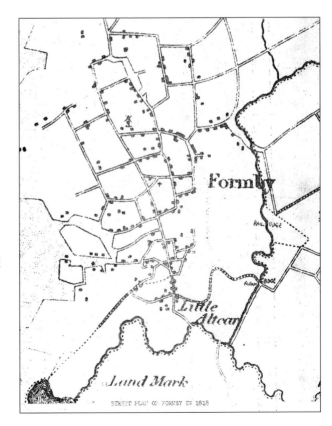

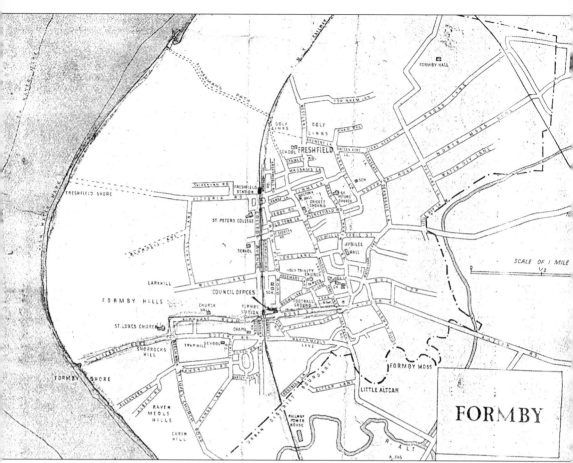

Street map of 1910, later amended to show the Council Offices, built in 1927. The hub of Formby as far as the road system is concerned was undoubtedly Cross Green, the site of the old village market fair and ancient cross. Here the main road from the south, having crossed the Alt and the original course of Downholland Brook (marked by the Formby/Altcar boundary), spreads like the branches of a tree in several different directions. There are also several lanes radiating off to the east and west from the site of the old church near the Kirklake. The map also shows the boundary of the newly established Urban District Council, which closely followed the boundary of the original parish, except that it no longer included Ainsdale. Instead the northern limit of the District is shown by a straight line running to the coast at Woodvale, north of Formby Hall.

Cross Green. The date of the original cross is not known. An oak cross 8ft 6in high stood here on a stone base for many years and was replaced by the present sandstone one in 1879. The old one, encased in lead, was then transferred to St Luke's churchyard where its steps are still to be seen. Legend has it that the Downholland Brook could flood to this point. Formby Fair, established in the fourteenth century, was held on the Green each year on Oak Apple Day, 29 June. Horses, cattle, sheep and pigs were sold. Nicholas Blundell of Crosby visited it with his wife in June 1710, together with Mr Anderson of Lydiate, Mr Blundell of Ince and his lady. In 1715 he records a stage play acted there. The Cross Green Inn, formerly the Blundell Arms, may have been preceded by an older beer house. Roselands, the large house, was used during the Second World War as a convalescent home for servicemen. For many years it has been used as a centre for the Red Cross and other voluntary organizations. Nearby, on the corner of Phillips Lane and Liverpool Road, were the village stocks and lock-up.

Church Road (incorrectly named on this postcard from the 1920s) was one of the original main routes through Formby. Going north from Cross Green, the road had few houses and as depicted here was well wooded. Next to the Bay Horse was Our Lady's School. It appears safe for children to cross – a far cry from the busy road of today.

Church Road, looking north. On the left is the new police station built by the Lancashire Constabulary in 1894. The land had been purchased from Revd Lonsdale Formby and John Formby, Esq. for the sum of £100. The building cost £2,074 4s. This building is still in use today. Opposite the police station and past the cottage was White House Farm. Here there was a milk herd and according to Mrs Sibley the milk was taken to Smithy Brow where it was cooled and then delivered in cans.

Wilson's Corner. On the corner is a typical wooden finger-post showing the main roads from this junction. The road to the left is Cable Street which led to Watchyard Lane and then out of Formby by the road over the Moss, making this a main route to Ormskirk. The shops were joined by a garage in 1910, the first in Formby, founded by Tom Wilson who came from Grange-over-Sands.

The imposing Moorhouse Building, on the corner of Old Mill Lane and Church Road. In the 1920s this was the Urban District Council Office. Complete with a lecture room and classrooms, this was where the council's Technical Classes were held. Verandas like this could be seen in other parts of Formby. Sadly they have all but disappeared.

Green Lane. To the north of St Peter's church, the road quickly became a country lane with a sandy surface and large untrimmed hedges. The small baby pram dates the photograph to around 1900.

Piercefield Road. The state of this important road continued to cause concern into the early twentieth century. All of the Formby roads and lanes would have been like this originally, as Catherine Jacson describes. To the right of the photograph is where the Embassy Cinema was subsequently constructed.

Old Town Lane. The village centre moved following the inundation of the old town near St Luke's church in the early eighteenth century and was then in the area of Timms Lane. Thus, Old Town Lane would have led back to the original old town. The shop shown on the right was Wilson's chemists, also a post office, who supplied veterinary medicines as well.

White Cottage, Gores Lane. This is probably one of the oldest Formby lanes at the heart of the seventeenth-century town. This thatched, whitewashed cottage standing with its gable facing the road is typical of many in the area. In 1953 Mr William Marshallsey, a local historian, calculated there were at least 49 similar cottages still inhabited. Many had been in continuous occupation by the same family for several generations. This was tenanted in 1846 by William Halewood. It is said to have had granary steps.

Old Mill Lane. The old post-mill, thought to date from the time of Henry VIII, stood here until 1885. This mill had a fixed conical turret of brick, above which the mill itself was turned on its central post. An interesting condition in the lease between the miller, Peter Travis, and Revd Richard Formby in 1772 was that the miller 'will sufficiently keep one pointer or other dog and that he sell to Richard Formby all the meal, seeds, bran, wheat and grain produced by the mill at the market price as demanded in Formby'.

Cottages on the corner of Old Mill Lane and Gores Lane. These buildings were severely damaged by a bomb in 1941. Like many in Formby their construction was based on a wooden cruck frame. Fortunately it was photographed and later depicted in embroidery showing its construction.

The Formby Embroidery. This is one of seventy-two embroidered illustrations which depict the history of Formby from the Vikings to the present day. It was designed and embroidered in the 1970s by Miss Lilian Rushton, a founder member of the Formby Society, who died in 1982. The final panels were completed by the local Guild of Embroiderers before the complete work was given by her sister to the Formby Society.

Reg Brown's Cottage. Almost opposite White Cottage on Gores Lane, this cottage was renovated and archaeologically examined in the early 1980s. This provided a unique opportunity to see and photograph the inside construction of the wooden beams.

Freshfield Road, from the top of Rosemary Lane, looking north. This is a very old road, depicted on old maps long before the railway was built. On the tithe map of 1845 the part from Brows Lane to Wicks Lane is called Fisherman's Lane and the rest Four-Acre Lane. The cottage on the right which had a large orchard behind was one of the last sites to be developed. A 'pound' stood opposite, for stray farm animals.

Rosemary Lane. This view, looking down from Freshfield Road, shows the lane surfaced with sets and bordered by overgrown hedges – it bears little resemblance to the road of today. The cottage on the left also backed onto an orchard and when demolished made way for the development of Lonsdale Road, started before the Second World War.

Duke Street. Photographed from Elbow Lane looking towards the Cross House inn, this view is still much the same today, apart from the traffic. Most of the houses at this end were built before the First World War. It was a convenient place to live, within walking distance of the village and station.

Thatched cottages in Duke Street. Walking towards the station from Elbow Lane, these cottages were on the north side of the road overlooking the area which became The Park. In the 1851 census the occupations of the inhabitants are given as fishermen or farmers. These cottages would have had large back gardens, used for growing vegetables.

Andrews Lane. This lane may have been one of the early routes to Little Crosby and then on to Liverpool. These substantial houses were built at the turn of the century. There was open space in front, but the road is still only a sandy track.

The late nineteenth-century brick-built houses on the south side of Queens Road had large gardens at the rear. There was nothing between these houses and the sea. The access way was down a sandy track with a stream on the north side with watercress growing on the banks; this is now under the pavement of Bushby's Lane with a few willow trees marking its path.

Formby Street. These houses were built in the late nineteenth century for commuters from Liverpool, who found them very convenient for the station. When erected there was no Station Hill at the end.

Ravenmeols Lane, here so free from traffic that people could cross easily. It was here in the late nineteenth century that Dr Gill built a private lunatic asylum, Shaftesbury House. It was set back from the road in extensive grounds and subsequently became a special school. Today the area is yet another new housing estate.

Ravenmeols Lane. Here were some small cottages with white-washed walls and thatched roofs, again inhabited by fishermen.

Tyrer's Cottage, Phillip's Lane. Here in the middle of the lane, which remained undeveloped until the 1960s, Mr John Tyrer had a nursery garden on land where his father had farmed. He supplied many people with shrubs and plants for their gardens. He subsequently sold the land for building and moved to Lydiate. His name lives on in Tyrer's Close, on the site of his land.

John Tyrer. Born in Formby in 1893, John attended St Luke's School. In his day, the school had ninety pupils, too many for the building, so the infants moved to the Formby Band's room in King's Road. John left school aged thirteen and helped his father before going on to develop his own nursery. During the Second World War he was ordered to grow fruit and vegetables, so concentrated on tomatoes. He recalled that a bomb dropped and 'messed up a lot of his fruit trees'. In 1957 he moved to Lydiate. He was a keen apiarist and lectured on bee-keeping and for many years he was a judge at the Formby Show. John lived to be 101. (Photograph courtesy of Mrs B. Tyler)

Dean's Cottage. This cottage once fronted onto Ravenmeols Lane but, having lost its front garden to new housing, now fronts on to Park Road, next door to Ravenmeols Community Centre. This is an original cruck cottage with outer walls made of local bricks. The clay for these probably came from near where Redgate School stands today. Note the sturdy wooden guttering and the sliding-sash windows typical of traditional local cottages.

Cockle Lane, Cheapside. This photograph taken from an old glass lantern slide shows a cottage in need of repair or demolition. Being without water supply or drainage such houses were often demolished but it is said it took days to burn the old thatch!

Moss Side. This route towards Ormskirk has hardly changed over the years. There are old cottages on the south side and then a bridge guarded by white rails. Further on at the Formby/Downholland boundary there is another bridge taking the road over Downholland Brook. Some time in the last century Downholland Brook was straightened here. At one time, one of the cottages near to the brook was an ale house called the Bridge Inn – very welcome for farmworkers and travellers over the Moss.

'Formby-by-the-Sea'. This was an enterprise by the Formby Land and Building Company which started in 1875 with a capital of £50,000. Despite construction of a promenade between 1876 and 1888, only a few houses were built. The nearest house in the picture was called Stella Maris, and the little boy on the foreshore is Philip Clulee, now a well-known local figure. The dual-level promenade was soon overwhelmed by blown sand. A railway loop was planned to connect with the main line at Hightown and Ainsdale and a station was to be sited behind the hotel. However, the necessary Act of Parliament did not succeed until after the impetus for the scheme was lost. (Photograph courtesy of M. Clulee)

Carrs Crescent. The more successful part of the Formby Land Company's development was the area nearest Eccles crossing, consisting of Elson Road, Carrs Crescent, Foster Road etc. Here some nice houses were built but plans to establish parks, boulevards, markets, laundries and winter gardens did not materialize.

'From the station gate', Victoria Road. When Harington Barracks was relinquished by the army in the early 1960s the site was acquired by New Ideal Homesteads Ltd. Their brochure included this view from Freshfield station bridge, showing Victoria Road. Before the housing development had been announced rumour had it that the site was going to be used for an open prison. The local councillors and MP acted quickly to prevent this.

THE SHORE↑

FORMBY GOLF COURSE ↓

ENTRANCE TO VICTORIA PARK ESTATE ↑

VICTORIA ROAD→

↑ FRESHFIELD STATION

Victoria Park Estate. This aerial view gives a good impression of the area which has developed over the past thirty years much as the planners envisaged. In the top left corner you can still see the army camp layout. The brochure states that in almost every case a garage or space for one car was intended. Perhaps it should have said 'space for two cars'. This new estate was one of many. There are now increased numbers of visitors to the pine woods, shore and squirrel reserve.

A natural history ramble along Wicks Lane in 1960. This ancient lane which runs from Freshfield Road to the shore follows the boundary between the Blundell estate to the north and Formby land to the south. The lane was cut by the railway and there used to be an unmanned level crossing where there is now a footbridge and then a few houses on the seaward side. Larkhill Farm was one of the last asparagus farms in the area. Three cast iron boundary markers are still to be found before the shore is reached. The final marker is now found in the inter-tidal zone on the foreshore.

The bypass, c. 1928. In 1930 Lancashire County Council agreed 'to eliminate no less than sixteen right-angle bends in a distance of $3\frac{1}{2}$ miles, build a new bridge over the Alt and to straighten all winding stretches, including bypassing the former main route through Formby'. Constructed over Formby Moss, this road was described in 1938 as 'a straight slash through virgin territory' and replaced one of the most dangerous stretches of the winding and treacherous main road from Liverpool to Southport. This soon carried a year-round stream of private cars and commercial traffic, swollen in the summer by holiday crowds.

The blacksmith. Every country village had at least one blacksmith. This forge may have been one in Little Altcar on Lunt Lane, remembered by older residents. There was, however, another in Watchyard Lane from which Smithy Green takes its name. Public notices are displayed about the 1871 Dog Act and the forthcoming Sports. It was an important focal point of village life.

Five

Planes, Trains and Automobiles

Freshfield shore provided one of the earliest flying strips in Britain. This picture dates from 1910 when there were only fifteen licensed pilots in the country. Five of them had planes and hangars at Freshfield.

Cecil Patterson. Flying commenced at Freshfield in May 1910 after Cecil Patterson, a Liverpool motor engineer and company director, had developed an ambition to fly. He bought a Farman biplane, in parts, at a cost of £625, and transported it by motor along the deserted lanes from Liverpool. He assembled it on the shore in an hour. Twenty minutes later, with six gallons of petrol aboard to power its 30hp engine, he flew at an altitude of 30ft for two or three hours. Patterson was the first aviator to succeed at his first attempt in an untried machine. Hangars were soon needed at Freshfield, to one of which he added a bedroom. Soon he was experimenting further and even giving lessons. On 23 June he had a minor crash but on August Bank Holiday, the damage having been repaired, he flew to Southport. He was soon flying every day, having marked out part of the shore (then privately owned) as an airstrip. He received his pilot's certificate in December 1910.

Another early aviator was Gerald Higginbotham from Macclesfield, who bought a used Blériot in a Manchester car salesroom for a knock-down price. He built himself a hangar, assembled his plane with instructions on two sheets of paper sent to him by Blériot and later the same morning was in the air. He was soon flying over the surprised captains of Atlantic liners in the Mersey.

W.D. Thomson's biplane. By the end of 1910 there were five aircraft at Freshfield. The two original fliers were joined by W.D. Thomson, a patent agent, who became the chairman of Liverpool Aeronautical Society and had one of Handley-Page's very first machines.

R.A. King, Patterson's pupil from Neston. He became the first passenger ever to cross the Mersey by air, with Patterson at the controls.

Shortly afterwards Henry Melly joined the other pilots at Freshfield in another Blériot with a 25hp engine, a copy of the plane which had crossed the Channel in 1909. Melly, aged forty-two, had just got married. He and his bride went to France on honeymoon and while there he took a nine-week flying course and obtained his licence, number 212. He spent about six months at Freshfield and early in 1911 moved to Waterloo which was his base as an instructor until flying stopped when war broke out in 1914. He had been told not to fly over gun emplacements on the shore. The Royal Naval Air Service took over his hangars.

Formby station, between 1904 and 1912. Because road communication between Liverpool and Southport was so difficult in the mid-nineteenth century, an Act of Parliament was passed in 1847 for the construction of a Liverpool, Crosby and Southport railway. The first sod was cut on 24 March 1847. The flat nature of the country facilitated quick and cheap construction and the formal opening took place in July of the following year. Formby was one of the original stations, a very modest affair with a level crossing at Duke Street. The station was replaced in around 1880 and this is the station shown here. It included a house for the stationmaster on the up platform. Note the footbridge where the road bridge was subsequently erected. Formby won the 'best-kept station garden' in the London Midland Region in1964, when people travelled to Formby especially to see it!

The railway was originally nicknamed the 'Shrimp Line'. Unfortunately the directors, who included Dr Richard Formby, knew little about running a railway. On one occasion in 1848 because of insufficient carriages passengers were reduced to riding on the tops of carriages and some even on the engine! In 1855 it was taken over by the Lancashire and Yorkshire Railway Company. Unfortunately, the LYRC was for many years one of the worst managed and most ill-equipped systems in the country and the railway became the object of scorn and derision. An overhaul was, however, finally achieved and things improved. In 1904 the line was electrified and became one of the pioneers of electric traction in the country. New rolling stock was bought which then served well until 1940.

The original Duke Street crossing. The Railway Hotel is to the left, out of the picture. To the right of the station bridge was a coal yard and the offices of the Formby Coal Company. In around 1912 the original level crossing and footbridge at Duke Street were replaced by the road bridge with station office on top, which survives today.

Eccles Crossing. This, the second Formby level crossing, still survives but in earlier days was supervised by a signal box. A goods siding alongside Andrews Lane is visible, as are the 'railway houses'. There was a light tramway from this siding to convey construction materials to the embryonic development of Formby-by-the-Sea at Albert Road.

An Edwardian view from the footbridge at Freshfield station, looking towards Southport. Freshfield station was opened in 1854. At that time there was little cultivation or development to the west of the line, there being nothing but sandy heath and dunes down to the shore. In the vicinity of the station a Mr Fresh had started farming and apparently a siding was used to unload manure. The name of Freshfield was then invented for this station and it is now applied to the northern part of Formby. The track was originally single from this point northward. The few local residents were provided with first-class passes for the first ten years of the life of the railway.

Station staff and passengers on the up platform at Freshfield. John F. Wetherall was ticket-collector. Following electrification, an intensive service of over seventy trains each day was introduced. In between there were 'through' steam trains between Southport and Liverpool Lime Street, with carriages to and from London. Before the First World War a 'Precedent' locomotive was stationed in the Lancashire and Yorkshire Railway shed at Southport to work this service. Tank engines were used for another half-century to haul goods trains, and the LYR 2.4.2 tank engine took over the through carriages. It was a steam engine that made the fastest ever run on the 'electric line'. A five-coach special on 15 July 1897 hauled by an Aspinall 4.4.2 'High-flyer' type is reputed to have reached the magic speed of 100mph. The operation of this express train over a basic line occupied by frequent local trains stopping at all stations must have posed a problem!

Woodvale station (Cheshire Lines Committee), 1944. Opened in 1884 as Woodville and Ainsdale, it was renamed Woodvale in 1898. It was temporarily disused for two years at the end of the Second World War and finally closed for good in 1952, the track to Southport subsequently becoming the Coastal Road of today. A steam engine is visible in the goods yard. Cavendish House, used as an officers' mess for Woodvale during the Second World War, can be clearly seen. Less obvious are the concrete blocks by the bridge to block it in case of invasion.

Hall Road was the site of a tragic accident which claimed the lives of many Formby people on 27 July 1905, involving an express train speeding towards Formby. A signalman put the preceding slow train into a siding. The following express from Liverpool was accidentally directed into the same siding, slamming into the back of the stationary train. Twenty-two people were killed. Fortunately, since then there have been few serious accidents on the line.

In order to provide electric power a large generating station was built by the side of the River Alt which supplied water for condensation purposes so that it was not necessary to build cooling towers. Power was obtained from sixteen Lancashire boilers driving cross compound steam engines. Ashes were disposed of on a narrow-gauge railway. It is said that the power generated here was also used in some Formby houses for a period. This power station continued in use until 1946. Afterwards current was supplied from Clarence Dock. A small 'halt' was provided on the railway for workers coming to and from Formby. During the Second World War, steam trains were again run in place of electric trains when power was unavailable and a special train service was run between Liverpool Central station and Southport by the railway committee between December 1940 and May 1941. On occasions there were interruptions of a few hours while bomb craters were filled in, rails relaid and trains had to pass at reduced speed until the ground had been consolidated.

The end of the steam era. Steam traction on this line was replaced by diesel in 1966 after a Black Five Stannier, no. 45146, pulled out on 15 April, 'with a final whistle of pride'.

Onward to Southport, passing the now dismantled signal box which controlled the National Coal Board siding. This nostalgic view of the last 'through carriages' direct from Euston would have prompted John Betjeman to write a poem!

Wilson's Garage. From left to right: Thomas Wilson, George Cobb, G. Lowe, Douglas Wilson, Richard Wilson, (Tom's father). The first garage in Formby was established by Tom Wilson in 1910. Born in 1884 at Grange-over-Sands, he served an engineering apprenticeship with Vickers-Armstrong in Barrow-in-Furness and subsequently sailed as a ship's engineer to South America. After arriving in Formby he did light engineering, agricultural and cycle repairs and even repaired the pioneer aircraft then flying from the shore.

Wedding fleet, 1939. Cyril Wilson, Tom's brother-in-law, and other drivers wait outside Our Lady's church. Mr Wilson, who was steeped in motoring history, handed the business over in 1950 to his son-in-law, Phil Clulee, who later established the Formby Coach Company as a separate business. Phil retired in 1982 when the business was sold to John Chapman and George Mawdsley who continue it to this day. (Photographs courtesy of Phil and Muriel Clulee)

Freshfield and District Motor and Cycle Company. In the 1920s the firm had new premises in Central Buildings, Church Road. Like the Formby Urban District Council offices in Moorhouse Buildings they also had a veranda. They advertised 'expert mechanics always in attendance for repairs and re-charging, cars for hire, petrol oils and greases.'

Turban Motors. This site, well known as a bus stop, was originally Parr's Garage until the 1950s, when it was taken over by Turner and Bancroft.

H. Woodward and Son. Their first garage premises were a disused army hut in Old Mill Lane, but they later moved to larger premises, the original Formby fire station, in Cable Street. The company was the area's main employer with 250 employees from Formby itself. From the beginning sand haulage was one of the main activities. By 1930 Noel Woodward was running a twelve-vehicle business and decided to move into new premises at the junction of the proposed new Formby bypass with Altcar Road. Erecting his new premises four years before work on the road began, Mr Woodward supplied all the materials required by the contractor. By 1938 Woodwards became the Leyland Group distributor for commercial vehicles in South Lancashire and North Cheshire. Agencies were also held for Austin, Triumph, Rover and Citroën cars. The company also constructed motor bodies and specialized in aluminium bodywork. Noel died in 1971 while still chairman of the company. The firm closed in December 1987.

An advertisement for Wilson's.

An advertisement for John W. Stevens.

Six

Sport and Recreation

Harold Creagh MIEE, Chief Electrical Engineer at Formby Power House, seen on his pony in Ravenmeols Lane in 1913. He lived in Formby for fifty-two years. Riding has always been a popular local pastime and there are many local stables and equine facilities.

An aerial view of the Formby Show. Run by the Formby Horticultural and Agricultural Society, it was described in its heyday as the largest one-day show in the country. It was first held in the 1880s and was well supported by local people; it was thought to be a great honour to be a prize winner.

FORMBY HORTICULTURAL SHOW 1911

The horticultural tent at the 1911 Formby Show. By this date the Show had become an established feature in Duke Street Park on the second Saturday of July. Most exhibits were under canvas, leaving the centre of the park for cattle showing, horse jumping and ring shows.

Lytles' display. Local authorities, market gardens and nurseries put on very extensive displays, a big effort for a one-day show. This display was from Lytles' Nurseries in Park Road. Mr Wright was another local rose grower who had nurseries in Halsall Lane and was a frequent exhibitor and prize winner as his father had been before him.

The children's tent. This became an important feature in the 1960s, when there would be up to 1,000 exhibits, including saucers of mustard and cress from children under five to flower-arrangements, dressmaking and woodwork from older children.

The Wine Society. This society always put on a colourful and topical display and won many top prizes. The Show continued in its old form until 1993, when there was a special two-day Show to celebrate its centenary. It included a procession through the village and finished with a firework display. The Show still continues but on a much reduced scale.

The Show Committee always tried to have an attractive ring show. Over the years these shows included displays by the Holcombe Hunt, displays by the Parachute Regiment and marching bands. At the hundredth show there was a display by horsemen dressed in the uniform of the 1880s, with ladies riding side-saddle.

Presentation of cups. All cups presented would be engraved with the name of the winner and the year. Here a cup is being presented to the winner in the Pony Class, one of the many classes judged in the ring on the day. This was followed by a Grand Parade of all competitors, complete with cups and rosettes.

The Picturedrome. In 1912 Monsignor Carr, Rector at Our Lady's church, was concerned that there was little to occupy young people in the evening, so he pressed for the Catholic Association Club House in Three Tuns Lane to be converted into a cinema. The 'Picturedrome', later to become the Queen's cinema, was opened on 21 December 1912. Tickets cost 3d, 6d and 1s. Electricity was obtained from a generator which also supplied several nearby houses. This had the disadvantage that the house lights went out when the cinema closed! The cinema finally closed in 1958 and is seen just before demolition.

The Embassy cinema. On 9 April 1932 a 'House of distinction of the cinema world' was opened. This building, built in 1928, had originally been a skating rink. Including decorative and stage lighting, there were four hundred lighting points. As in all cinemas of that time secondary lighting was by gas. The Embassy remained open until 1962, the last cinema to be open in the district around Southport.

A tournament at Formby Golf Club, 1967. The club was founded on the initiative of John Bushby in December 1884. It was decided to limit the membership to twenty-five local residents and to play on the fields of a local farm during the winter months. The club prospered, with Richard Formby Jnr as its first president. The first clubhouse was burned down in 1899 but was replaced by a bigger and better building, including dormitory accommodation for nine golfers, which opened in 1901.

The clubhouse of Freshfield Golf Club (or, more correctly, the Banking and Insurance Golf Club). The sandy dunes and heaths of south-west Lancashire have over the years produced excellent golf courses. Many are still flourishing after many years use but one that had a limited life was Freshfield Golf Club. This was north of Freshfield station and east of the railway line.

Greens and bunkers on Freshfield golf course. During the Second World War the land was requisitioned to make RAF Woodvale and the clubhouse became a Polish officers' mess. After the war the clubhouse was demolished but the foundations can still be seen.

Lifeboat House Café. Formby shore has aways attracted local people and day trippers as a place for relaxation, a pleasant walk, paddle or swim. At the end of Lifeboat Road the old boathouse was converted into a café and at one time there was an area where cycles could be safely left.

The Pine Tree Café, 1930s. There was also a café at the end of Victoria Road, a welcome sight for the many people who travelled to Freshfield by train and walked to the shore. Due to coastal erosion during the last twenty years this area has now been reclaimed by the sea.

Camping Rules. During the First and Second World Wars there were several camp sites in the area. One of the most popular was on Kirklake Road at the bottom of Station Hill, which extended to the back of what was then the last house in Wicks Lane where Mr and Mrs Criddle lived. Judging by these rules, campers in the area must have been well organized, which is more than can be said for Mr Criddle's donkey. If she was left out at night she would bray loudly and next day would be found surrounded by empty beer bottles!

1938.

WALKER'S CAMPING GROUND.

KIRKLAKE ROAD, FORMBY.

RULES.

1. **Campers** are charged 1/- per head (water included).
2. **Tents** left up unoccupied are charged 1/- per week.
3. **No** singing, music or other noises after 11 p.m.
4. **No** subletting of tents without permission.
5. **No** trespassing or damaging fences.
6. **Campers** must be suitably dressed on the Ground or on the road.
7. **The** only entrance and exit to the Ground is by the gate in Kirklake Road.
8. **No** obscene language.
9. **No** dogs allowed on the Ground.
10. **Litter** to be put in bins, and not thrown about.
11. **Dirty Water** must be thrown in the grid provided, and not about the Ground.
12. **This Camp** is Licensed. These Rules must be strictly adhered to.

E. WALKER.

Formby caravan site. Today Formby has two caravan sites, including this one to the south of Lifeboat Road where sand has been removed, leaving a large flat area. This developed from a rather primitive site in the late 1940s to today's site with full facilities.

An aerial view of Freshfield caravan site. The caravan site at the end of Victoria Road had to be resited further inland in 1970 when it was in danger of being overcome by blown sand. This photograph also shows Jimmy Lowe's asparagus fields and the Freshfield navigational landmark which was claimed by the sea in the late 1960s. (Photograph courtesy of John Houston)

Since the 1960s public access to the beach, dunes and woodlands has dramatically increased. The asparagus fields have now been replaced by car parking for visitors. The average number of visitors on summer Sundays is now over 3,000. Dune management and access control introduced by the Sefton Coastal Management Scheme since the 1970s are directed at controlling the inevitable environmental damage caused. Here a board-walk is being constructed at the National Trust reserve in 1983.

The records of the Formby Lawn Tennis Club are very sparse but it appears that in 1896 the Reverend Lonsdale Formby (vicar of St Peter's) gave land for the establishment of a cricket field and lawn tennis ground between Gores Lane and Green Lane. This picture was taken at the second annual tennis match between the tennis and cricket clubs in 1950. Mr W.H. Lister of Formby CC is playing Mr Hawkins, of the Tennis Club. Also in the picture are Miss Mary Creagh, Miss J. Rigby and Alan Mills, who later became a Wimbledon referee.

Members of Formby Tennis Club relax outside the clubhouse in Gores Lane. Today the club has four floodlit hard courts, five grass courts and over five hundred members. Each year it holds a Family Tournament when all members of the family can show their prowess or support husbands, wives and children.

Formby Cricket Club. The Cricket Path has been the spiritual home of cricket in Formby since 1865 and was very advanced for its time when in 1920 it decided to admit women as playing members and provide a separate (smaller) pavilion for them. Apparently this initiative did not come to fruition but the club has since gone from strength to strength. Here, Lancashire 2nd XI walk onto the pitch in August 1966.

Formby Athletic Football Club. Photographed in 1909, this could be the first Formby football team. Names of some of the players are: W. Holden, Ivor Morgan, A. Holden, J. Rimmer and Bob Wright. This was long before the construction of today's football ground or the park, so the pitch was probably lent by a friendly farmer.

Formby Theatre Club. Founded just after the Second World War, the club, originally the Fellowship Players Dramatic Society, presented two plays a year in Holy Trinity parish hall. Rehearsals were held in the tennis pavilion and later in an ex-Army Cadet hut. Today they have purpose-built premises. One of the first productions was *Flarepath* in 1947.

In the early 1950s members of the Formby Theatre Club included seventeen-year-old Beryl Bainbridge, seen here on the left at a fancy-dress party. Other past members of the society include Adrian Mills who appeared in *That's Life* for the BBC and Lesley Sharpe who appeared with the Royal Shakespeare Company. Others included in this picture are Janet Drummond, Kath Williams and Minnie Drummond.

The Freshfield Bowling Club. During the First World War the club played host to convalescent soldiers. Always known locally as the 'Tin-tab', allegedly because of its origins as a corrugated-iron mission-room, it was formally opened in May 1894 by Mr John Formby. The original green was laid at a cost of £67 and prizes at the first event were a clock, a silver-plated teapot and a basket of ducklings.

The 1st Formby Scout Troop, 1909. The troop was formed in that year, just one month after Lord Baden-Powell had founded the Scout movement. Their leader was Mr Murray Spence (in the centre, with moustache), who lived at Glen Lyon, Freshfield Road; their chaplain (on the right), was Revd J.B. Richardson, vicar of Holy Trinity. Other officers were Dr Stanley Gill of Shaftesbury House and Musketry Instructor R. Heywood of Laurd House, College Avenue. The flag being proudly displayed was hand-made by Mrs Atkinson and is still in use today.

The Bay Horse pub. This hostelry was built around 1860 and its first licensee was John Dickinson, brewer, farmer and beer-seller. The original house was the left-hand part of the present building with its front door in the centre. Two rooms were on either side of a narrow passage and the very small bar was at the rear of the left hand room. The tap room was behind this, as were the living quarters for the licensee and his family. A pump and trough still stand at the original right-hand corner of the house. Changes started in 1956 when landlord Robert Whitehead added the lounge bar and named it the Fullerton Lounge after the triple Waterloo Cup winner. The same year the Withens Lounge was built and the car park was extended over a field previously used by visiting fairs and for Home Guard practice. The Carvery area which replaced the Withens was built in 1983. The striking weeping ash which stands at the south-east corner of the building is remembered by those who were children here during the Second World War as the 'gum tree', due to an association with visiting American airmen.

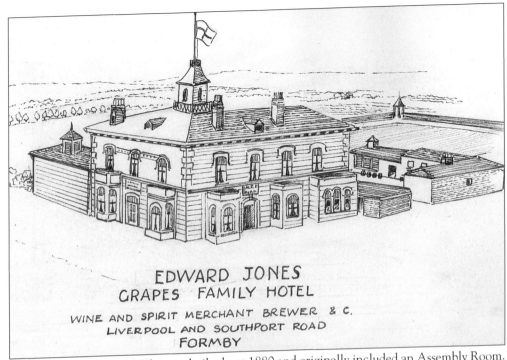

EDWARD JONES
GRAPES FAMILY HOTEL
WINE AND SPIRIT MERCHANT BREWER & C.
LIVERPOOL AND SOUTHPORT ROAD
FORMBY

The Grapes family hotel. This was built about 1880 and originally included an Assembly Room. In 1883 seventy members of the Naturalists' Field Club travelled from Exchange Station to Freshfield and a local newspaper reported: 'After wandering in a desert [they] met at the Grapes Family Hotel where tea was served in a handsome room. The proverbial purity of the Formby air on an exceptionally fine day made the excursion highly enjoyable. Mr Jones calls himself a wine and spirit merchant and brewer.' The buildings on the right are probably the brew-house.

The Royal Hotel. This pub has long been a meeting place for people living in the area. During wartime the soldiers stationed at Altcar left their names scratched for posterity on a glass window, which survived until a recent renovation. In 1890 when the lifeboat crew wished to write to the Dock Committee they wrote from the Royal Hotel. The Reciprocity Brewery buildings, which still stand today at the rear of the building, can be seen on old maps. Greyhound racing used to take place on the fields behind the pub.

The Railway Hotel was built in 1848, at the same time that the railway itself was constructed. Adjacent to it there was a level crossing and the stationmaster's house. Both of these disappeared when Station Hill was built in 1912. At the back of the hotel there was a bowling green but like most of the greens attached to pubs it was made into a car park in the 1970s. In its early days it sold locally brewed beer. A small building on the west side was once used as a temporary mortuary when several bodies were washed up on the shore.

The Blundell Arms. This is now better known by its original name of the Cross House Inn. It overlooks the village green where fairs were held and proclamations made and may well have been preceded by an earlier, smaller beerhouse. It was at the Blundell Arms that the last meetings of the ancient Manor Court, the Court Leet, were held in the early years of this century. It had a beautiful bowling green and a commodious range of stables and other outbuildings which have now made way for the car park.

The Waterloo Cup. In 1825 Viscount Molyneux founded the Altcar Cup on his father's estate at Altcar. The Waterloo Cup, the Grand National of coursing, was founded in 1836 at the instigation of William Lynn in whose hotel, the Waterloo, the owners dined on the eve of their meetings. As the years passed, the Lords Sefton took an increasing interest in the Waterloo cup and its administration so that they became regarded as the uncrowned Royal Family of coursing. (Reproduced courtesy of NMAG, Merseyside)

Going to Altcar. Coursing is said to have existed as a sport for some 4,000 years. It was probably introduced to this country after the Norman Conquest. Since then it has been as keenly pursued as the hare itself in the more rural corners of the countryside. Participation here in Formby has traditionally been popular. For many small farmers and breeders, going to Altcar in style in a veteran horse-drawn conveyance would be one of the highlights of the year. All would need to be well wrapped up, as coursing at Altcar has been described as one of the coldest sports in the world!

Seven

Wreck and Rescue

A beachmark. Whether or not Formby ever had a 'port' itself in historical times is still debated but the Mersey has for a considerable time been an important seaway for the many thousands of vessels which have plied to and from the port of Liverpool. Many attempts have been made since the eighteenth century to make navigation of the channels safer but early methods were primitive and not surprisingly many ships ran aground. Records show that between 1745 and 1946 over three hundred vessels came to grief on the sandbanks between Waterloo and Ribble.

A panel of the Formby Tapestry depicting Viking ships and settlers. This scene may have taken its inspiration from the raven-headed prow of a Viking long-ship, discovered in a local garden in the late 1930s. After being examined by experts it was presented to Liverpool Museum but sadly perished in the Blitz of 1941. (Embroidery by Lillian Rushton)

Q2 Buoy. The main channels into the port, originally including the Formby Channel, were marked by buoys from the mid-eighteenth century. These were supplemented by light-vessels stationed at strategic points. In severe storms even these vessels were not safe and occasionally lost their moorings.

Formby Lighthouse, built on the bank of the River Alt, just seaward of where the railway crosses the Alt today. It started as a landmark in 1719 being converted in 1834 at a cost of £40 into a lighthouse with a cottage added for the keeper. Its lighthouse days were short, being replaced by Crosby lighthouse in 1839, but it remained a local landmark until blown up in 1941 so as not to guide German bombers as it had guided shipping for over two hundred years.

The wreck of the *Henry J. Smith*, 1916. The four-masted schooner, registered in New York, was being towed by tug into Liverpool when the tow-rope parted and she drifted on to Freshfield shore. Four lifeboats went to her assistance. The crew walked ashore but the ship broke her back. The disaster was photographed by bird-watcher F.W. Holder.

Still one of the most prominent wrecks is that of the *Ionic Star* whose mast rears out of the water over Mad Wharf. This ship carrying a cargo of fruit, cotton and meat came aground in thick fog on 17 October 1939. The remaining sections were used for target practice in 1942 when they were bombarded by mortars and field guns, but may still be seen. (Photograph courtesy of J. Rathbone)

Formby Lifeboat Station was established by Liverpool Dock committee in 1776 and was the first in Great Britain. The boathouse overlooked the main shipping channel into the port. Over the years the lifeboat was replaced several times. Most of the boats were designed and built by a local boat builder, Thomas Costain. This one, the penultimate boat, was launched in 1874 and cost £265. The coxswain, Henry Aindow, was one of the survivors of a disaster in 1836 when the lifeboat capsized with the loss of five crew members, including Lt Walker, the lighthouse keeper.

The 'Lifeboat' Aindows. John Aindow stands with his wife, Catherine, his daughter and four sons. It is claimed that at one stage the Boat was crewed entirely by Aindows or their relations and the Lifeboat House was 'home'.

Mr John Aindow, coxswain. He served forty-eight years in the crew, twenty-five as coxswain following his father from 1885, at a salary of £7 10s per year. He retired at the age of seventy-one. In his crew he numbered five sons and five nephews. On his retirement in 1910 he received a framed testimonial, the silver medal of the Liverpool Shipwreck and Humane Society and a 'purse of gold'. Several generations of Aindows were brought up in the Lifeboat House.

The *John and Henrietta*. Provided by an anonymous donor after the station had been taken over by the RNLI, the last boat was commissioned in 1896 with John Aindow Snr, as cox. 'Tippings' plates' on the carriage wheels prevented them sinking into the soft sand. The carriage allowed paired horses. The boathouse shows its new frontage with a lookout, erected in 1892.

The last launch of the *John and Henrietta*. Because of wartime difficulties in 1916, the boat was launched with the aid of locally based troops from Altcar.

After the closure of the lifeboat station in 1918, the sandhills freely encroached and surrounded the building, which for many years was used as a tea-room. John Aindow Jnr remained, however, at Lifeboat Cottage behind the station to read the tide poles every fifteen minutes until he in turn handed over his duties to Joseph Aindow who left the cottage on its demolition. It was dismantled at the same time as the Boathouse in 1965.

Coastguard lookout, 1970s. The Divisional Rescue Coastguard Headquarters first moved from Hoylake to Formby in 1949 in order to provide a better position to observe the sea traffic moving up the Mersey. They originally had a timber and glass building situated north of the lifeboat station. This was replaced by a bigger and better brick and timber structure at the end of Albert Road. (Photograph by Harry Bevan)

View from the senior watch-officer's position in the Coastguard lookout. This was near the remains of Stella Maris, a house which had been used as a radar station during the Second World War. In 1975, because of the accretion of sand dunes restricting the view, the lookout had to be re-sited again and it was then decided to rebuild it at Hall Road. (Photograph by Bob Wagstaff)

Coastguard J. Rigby watching ship movements in the 1970s. Rescue, lookout and reporting remained the three main functions. While telephone and radio communications were becoming increasingly important, telescopic vigilance and observation remained necessary in Liverpool Bay. Beach patrols and use of life-saving equipment was also included.

The prize-winning Coastguard team in 1949/50. From left to right: Cdr Bartlet, Jeff Aindow, Inspector A. Shaw; behind: C.G. Lydiate, A/C E. Peel. (Photograph courtesy of Bob Wagstaff)

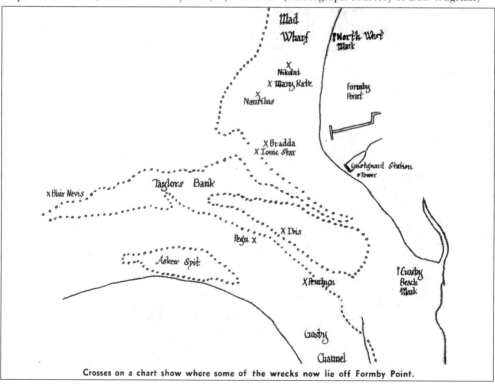

Crosses on a chart show where some of the wrecks now lie off Formby Point.

Wreck chart. There are approximately eighty wrecked ships on the banks and coast between the Ribble and the Mersey. Famous wrecks include the Manx coaster *Brada* which capsized off Formby in 1936. In 1939 the steamer *Pegu* was stranded on the east bank of the Formby Channel and broke her back, carrying a valuable cargo including Scotch whisky. This produced a situation similar to that in *Whisky Galore*.

Eight

Formby's
Proud War Record

Over the last hundred years or so, Formby men and women have served their country in a variety of ways during at least three major conflicts. At the start of the century the Boer War was being fiercely fought in South Africa. These men of D Company (Formby), 3rd Volunteer Battalion of the King's (Liverpool) Regiment, photographed in 1900, were about to depart for South Africa. In the days before radio news travelled slowly and each week the newspapers were anxiously scanned by relatives for details of casualties.

'It's a long, long way to Tipperary'. The words of this song may well have been on the lips of these soldiers on parade in a Formby street in 1914. In disgust at the conduct of the war, the poet Siegfried Sassoon is said to have thrown his Military Cross in the sea at Formby.

The Second World War directly involved civilians for the first time and Formby was no exception. This fine body of men, photographed in 1943, was Formby's own 'Dad's Army', or Home Guard. Their duties included one all-night spell a week manning anti-aircraft guns at Seaforth. Mr Garret Lacey is featured second from the left on the back row.

The King's Regiment depot rugby team in 1943, with their Commanding Officer, Lt-Col. Burke Gaffney MC. He commanded Harington Barracks from 1941 to 1945 and soon established a good relationship with the local residents. The War Office originally planned to take over the golf club and its land for training purposes but fortunately a less drastic course was followed. The CO subsequently became Colonel of the Regiment and wrote the official history of the modern regiment. (Photograph courtesy of Austen Cartmel)

Mounting Guard, 1946. Many thousands of now middle-aged men will be able to remember their first six weeks' primary training at Harington Barracks before being posted to their definitive regiment. The old depot of the King's (Liverpool) Regiment at Seaforth became inadequate as recruits began to flow in after the outbreak of war in 1939 and so was moved eight miles north to the 'hutted camp' sited on open farmland in Formby. This became the King's Regiment Infantry Training Centre and continued in the early part of the war to receive 200 recruits every fortnight. (Photograph courtesy Austen Cartmel)

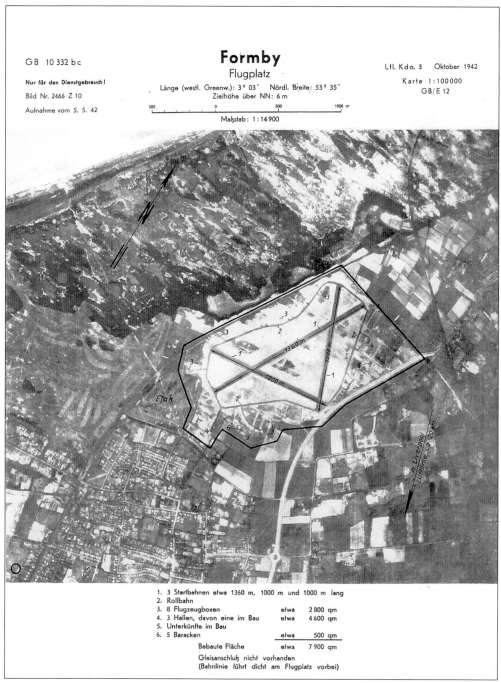

An enemy aerial photograph of Woodvale, 1942. During this Luftwaffe reconnaissance early in 1941, it seems that no-one on the ground was aware of the enemy aircraft in the clear sky immediately above. The map shows that the Germans thought there was an anti-aircraft gun at Fisherman's Path but apparently this was not so.

A Polish Spitfire squadron. Twelve Spitfires of 315 Squadron fly in practice formation over Woodvale in 1942. Convoy patrols in the Irish Sea were one of the main duties of Woodvale squadrons, providing cover against enemy attack and reconnaissance against submarines. Practically, blowing sand was the most disruptive element. The first German aircraft was claimed on 3 May 1942.

Woodvale control tower. New Bronk Farm, the old farmhouse, originally surrounded by rabbit warrens but now surrounded by fighter planes, continued in use next to the control tower, providing accommodation for radio repair personnel until being pulled down in the 1970s. Note the landing-strip map on the wall, which was reinstated in the early 1990s and may still be seen. (Photograph courtesy of A. Ferguson)

256 Squadron, who were supplied with Mosquitoes in January 1943. A purpose-built operations room was opened in Broad Lane, covering some 300 miles of coastline. Providing round-the-clock day and night fighter cover needed a great number of personnel. Much of the accommodation, particularly for female personnel, was beyond the edge of the station. Some of these buildings remained after the war and were used by local farmers. The WAAF accommodation was subsequently inhabited by local people until proper housing could be built in the post-war period. The operations room is still in existence. (Photograph courtesy of A. Ferguson)

Stella Maris, Promenade Hotel, during the 1930s. This house on Formby promenade, with a flat roof and facing the sea, was selected in October 1940 to be a Chain Home Low Radar to defend Liverpool Bay. In view of its strategic position it had particular value in the defence of the western approaches to Liverpool. This role could not have been guessed at when this picture was taken! (Photograph courtesy of J. Rathbone)

RAF radar personnel on the roof of Stella Maris, 1941. Formby aerial plots would have been passed to the local fighter group and shipping plots to the naval plotting room in Liverpool. During the Battle of the Atlantic, Formby was chosen to be upgraded and the transmitter power was increased. The Royal Navy took over when the RAF left. Operational records of the station have survived in a special archive. Radar stations like this gave warning that could not have been obtained by any other means.

Formby radar station, Stella Maris, 1941. This was fortuitously photographed when a local family was returning from the foreshore with their pony cart laden with driftwood. Several weeks later and for the rest of the war, the station was unapproachable as it was surrounded by barbed wire. (Photograph courtesy of J. Rathbone)

Rifle training at Altcar Rifle Range. A rifle range was established at Balling's Wharf on Lord Sefton's land in 1862 by the 5th Lancashire Rifle Volunteers. In 1913 the land was transferred to the West Lancashire Territorial Association. Since then many thousands of soldiers have learnt their rifle skills at Altcar. (Photograph courtesy of Lt-Col. Michael Cook MBE, TD)

The control bunker for the 'Starfish' decoy, Range Lane. This undercover wartime project was not publicly known about until 1998. The bunker was the control centre for an elaborate electric decoy system which was switched on in the event of enemy attack to lure German bombers away from Liverpool and instead drop their lethal cargo on Ravenmeols sand-dunes. As bombs dropped, oil fires were started to simulate huge explosions. Bombs did in fact fall on Formby and in April 1941 started a major fire in the woodland near Formby Golf Club. Starfish was the codename for this web of decoy lights.

Observer Corps, November 1939. Their post was on the bank of the River Alt by the Altcar Road. (Photograph courtesy of Muriel Clulee)

Tom Wilson and F. Flatman of the Observer Corps, 1939. (Photograph courtesy of Muriel Clulee)

The Wings for Victory parade passing along Kings Road, 17 April 1943. (Photograph by F.S.)

As a precaution against the risk of invasion during the Second World War much of the shore from Southport to Crosby had to have poles planted as a defence against aerial attack. Here the young Tom Moss, later to become headmaster of a local school, plays with his bucket and spade among the wooden posts at the beginning of the war.

Nine

The Historical Landscape

An exposure of Downholland Silt at Formby Point. The several major prehistoric invasions by the sea of the south-west Lancashire coast can be traced by the layers of silt which extend beneath the land from their current exposure on the foreshore, seen here, inland as far as what has been described in the past as the 'Hillhouse coastline' on the far side of Downholland Moss. From this it can be seen that the sea has seriously inundated the land locally on five or six occasions in the last 9,000 years – the coastline is always on the move.

The 'Hamilton' map. Drawn by William Hamilton, Surveyor to the Duchy of Lancaster, this mid-sixteenth-century map (of which a copy is exhibited in Formby Library) was drawn to help settle a dispute over rights to dig peat and pasture cattle on parts of the 4,000 acres of marsh to the east of Formby, on the boundary between Formby, Halsall and Altcar. Formby is shown at the top right, adjacent to the River Alt. Among Formby's main topographical features, Formby church on the site of today's St Luke's church is shown. This was subsequently destroyed in the eighteenth century. The site of the 'Old Town' is shown close to the church, in the lee of the dunes, which subsequently overwhelmed it. Between this and the river is a 'Ferny-delph', thought to be in the ancient Manor of Ravenmeols. To the east is the 'Reed Pol,' a reedy pool, near where Redgate is today together with the 'Old Mill'. A New Mill is also marked near the bridge over Downholland Brook, near the present-day Tesco store. Between this and Altcar is a marshy area where geese were kept, (the 'Gorsedge') and also the 'Scaling', a summer pasture on the edge of the Moss. The Moss itself was obviously very marshy but also very fertile and full of wild flowers and watery pools. (Map re-drawn by Ted Turner)

Formby Hall. This old house is thought to date from the mid-sixteenth century. It came close to destruction in the mid-1970s but has now been lovingly restored by its new owner with advice from English Heritage. The home of the Formby family for four centuries, it had a 'face-lift' in the early nineteenth century when its front elevation was changed to the then fashionable 'Strawberry-Hill' neo-Gothic style, with added battlements and stucco façade. The Formby family, said to be descended from Albinus the Priest, owned one quarter of Formby land. The other three quarters had been owned originally by the Halsall family. When 'Bad Sir Henry' Halsall lost his fortune, the Blundells of Ince Blundell purchased the estate and so became the area's leading landowners until the mid-1960s. Other interesting features of the Hall's grounds are the ancient dovecote, still relatively intact, the small outbuilding used as a girls' school for a period and the fish-pond.

Ince Blundell Hall. This was built by Squire Henry Blundell, between 1720 and 1750. He became a collector, traveller and connoisseur. It stands in a deer park surrounded by a brick wall pierced by several imposing gates. Attached to the house is the Italianate Roman Catholic church of 1858 which now serves as the parish church. Nearby is the previous Old Hall, the ancient Cross Barn which served for religious use in the 'penal years' and a circular eighteenth-century priest's house. Henry Blundell added a 'Pantheon', a miniature version of the original in Rome, to hold some of his classical sculpture, and two small classical temples.

A manorial boundary stone. This old boundary marker was exposed on the high tide-line north of the old lifeboat house in the 1970s and had marked the coastal extremity of the ancient boundary between Formby and Ravenmeols. Ravenmeols was an independent township at the time of the Domesday survey. The coastal marshes were used for pasture by the monastic grange at Altcar for many years up to the Dissolution. Ravenmeols appears to have been largely lost to erosion during medieval times. John Formby purchased the Manor in 1757.

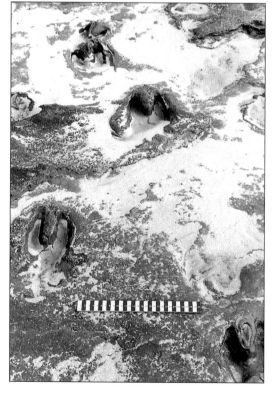

Fossilized footprints of an auroch. Each successive tide and storm strips more sand away from the beach. This erosion leaves bare the prehistoric silts beneath the sand which incredibly still bear the imprints of animal and human feet from six thousand years ago. Retired local schoolmaster Gordon Roberts has made a special study of them and as a result they have now been recognized nationally as an extremely rare form of archaeological record of long-extinct aurochs (primitive cattle) and also deer, wild boar, cranes and humans. There is only one other such site in the UK, in South Wales. (Photograph courtesy of Gordon Roberts)

Floodgates on the River Alt. Because of the low level of the Alt as it runs to the sea, it was tidal as far as Aintree until the Middle Ages and so liable to flooding. Constructed in 1830, these floodgates replaced ones at Altmouth. The originals had been constructed by the Monks from Stanlowe in the thirteenth century. They also erected a water-mill.

Altmouth Pumping Station. Following campaigns by local farmers, in 1968 work started on one of the country's largest pumping stations near the mouth of the Alt, 200ft upstream of the old tidal sluice gates seen above. This station opened in 1972 with a pumping capacity of over 1 million gallons a minute. Most of the time water is pumped out more slowly than this! (Photograph courtesy of the Environment Agency)

Altcar Pumping Station, 1972. The first pumping station on the Alt was a windmill pump established by Lord Sefton in around 1800 to drain his lands. This was replaced by a steam engine in 1842 but the windmill continued to stand alongside for some fifty years. The notable landmark of the chimney was demolished in 1919 when the station converted from coal to anthracite-oil fuel. On at least two occasions this chimney was struck by lightning. (Photograph courtesy of the Environment Agency)

Dune erosion. During recent years, this long sandy belt of dunes around Formby Point, with its unique flora and fauna, has been threatened by erosion. Efforts to hinder it by means of the planting of marram grass (which was an obligation on tenants in the past) has been fairly successful. Plantation of pines has also been tried but with less success. It is now seen that the natural mobility of the coast can not be halted except at unacceptable environmental and financial cost. Destruction of dunes has also occurred during the last half-century by sand-winning and tipping of nicotine waste.

Firwood. In the late eighteenth century, the Revd Richard Formby of Formby Hall became the first landowner on the Lancashire coast to experiment with plantations of trees using Scotch fir, sycamore, plane and ash at Firwood and then at Shorrocks Hill. One hundred years later an enthusiastic visitor commented on the success of the Formby plantations and the then landowner, Mr Weld-Blundell, was persuaded to try something similar. This he did, extensively, south from Woodvale using mainly Corsican pine as this had proved more successful in a similar hostile environment on the French Atlantic coast.

The National Trust Squirrel Reserve. Corsican pines, planted mainly in the early twentieth century partly to shelter the asparagus fields and partly as a cash crop, have suffered from the strong prevailing salt-laden winds, particularly on the frontal dunes where they have not succeeded in preventing erosion. They are, however, the home of our unusual colony of red squirrels. Legend has it that in around 1940 a local resident was asked to look after some Scandinavian red squirrels for a friend. This he duly did until one day they escaped and established the colony which is now so popular with visiting children. The reserve was acquired by the National Trust in 1965.

A Formby oil well. 1949

Oil wells on Formby Moss. During a geological survey of the area in 1939 a number of active seepages of petroleum were discovered. The oil found was of very good quality and a small but steady supply was soon being produced. Eight small pumps in fields on either side of Old Moss Lane were locally known as 'nodding donkeys'. By the 1960s they were still producing up to fifteen barrels of oil a week, having produced two and a half million gallons since 1939. Some is said to have found its way into the 'Pluto' pipeline which supplied oil to the liberation armies in Europe during the Second World War. Eventually the wells became uneconomic; the pumps were dismantled and removed. (Drawing by Muriel Sibley, 1949)

Poverty Fields. The naturally thin grassland and warrens around the present-day site of Freshfield station were too poor in their natural state for cultivation and this led to the title of 'Poverty Fields'. Until the mid-nineteenth century the lands west of the railway line were entirely uncultivated, but the rabbits they produced were an important contribution to the rural economy and their breeding grounds were carefully guarded and fenced. A Mr Fresh, realising that fertilizing the land would make it more productive, brought manure by train to his railway siding at Freshfield. This was 'night-soil' from Liverpool which had to be disposed of by rail and canal for agricultural use.

Jimmy Lowe, 'the Asparagus King', who had extensive fields at Victoria Road, is seen here with the first prize, a silver Challenge Cup, for his excellent asparagus at the Vale of Evesham on 30 May 1930. Formby's sandy fields when enriched with manure became ideal for growing asparagus and this delicacy became one of the area's claims to fame, even in London and on the Atlantic liners. It is said to have been introduced to Formby by the Formby family with seed brought from France. The subsequent coastal Corsican pine tree planting seems to have been designed to protect these fields. After the Second World War, asparagus farming never regained the momentum of its golden days. Only one asparagus farm still survives, the last remnant of a local tradition. (Photograph courtesy of Mrs J. Castle)

Kirklake Bank. The Kirk Lake was originally a wet slack in the lee of the sand dunes near the ancient Formby chapel. On the bank of this marshy ground this house was built by Dr Richard Formby MD for his daughter in around 1864. The house is said to have been a copy of a previous one in Aigburth which Dr Formby had lived in. There were complaints about the still unsurfaced road at the time the Urban District Council came into existence in 1905. Open fields to the rear of the house were being farmed for asparagus in the 1890s. They continued in cultivation until houses were built there in the 1970s.

'Death-duty Hill'. The large dunes seaward of St Luke's church were known originally as Shorrocks Hill and Beacon Hill. A lantern was hoisted on a mast there when the lifeboat crew were needed, as before the trees were planted it was visible from the village. These dunes were one of the earliest victims of sand winning. This started when John Formby found he had death duties to pay in the late 1920s. He funded the tax by agreeing to the extraction of sand at sixpence per ton. This was carted away by Noel Woodward. Sand-winning continued from behind the frontal dunes at many different sites and with other hauliers until the 1960s.

The 'Man-made Lake'. After various other sand-winning sites were exhausted the excavators returned to the area west of Atherton cottage and Greenloons Farm in 1966 and removed sand to such a level that a damp declivity was left, adjacent to Wicks Lane path. Following restoration work co-ordinated by the Merseyside County Council and funded by the Manpower Services Commission, the landscaped area known today as the 'man-made lake' was produced. The Sefton Coastal Management Scheme has now produced a very comprehensive and forward-looking management programme for the whole coastal strip. (Photograph courtesy of J. Houston)

Freshfield Slacks. These are low-level areas formed among the sand dunes by wind erosion. When the level of the water table, known locally as the Ream, is reached, a level area is produced and this remains until overwhelmed by the next invasion of a mobile sand dune. These slacks tend to flood during the winter months. They attract a particular flora and fauna quite distinct from the dunes and it is this which has made the Freshfield and Ainsdale dune system nationally known to natural historians since the nineteenth century. The area is now a National Nature Reserve. Unfortunately because of a drop in the level of the water table, the slacks have recently tended to dry out, with a consequent serious threat to indigenous flora and fauna. English Nature has been working on the site since 1965. (Photograph courtesy of English Nature)

Professor Tom and Mrs Edith Kelly were founder members of the Formby Society. They came to Formby in 1949, first living in Carr's Crescent and later Freshfield Road before retiring to Keswick in 1975. They both served terms of office as chairman of the Society and shared a particular interest in local history. They were both historians and had the ability to interest and stimulate the wide and varied membership of the History Group. Edith Kelly edited and was the chief contributor to *Viking Village*, first published in 1973. The third edition published in 1982 has long been out of print.

Formby War Memorial. This beautiful, central site was given by Mr C.J. Weld-Blundell in 1922 and records the names of 120 local people who died for their country in the First World War, including one woman, Jane Murray. Behind the cross is the further memorial to the sixty-eight people who gave their lives in the Second World War. The memorial became a cause célèbre in 1975 when the council drew up a development plan which envisaged removing it to a less favourable position. Miss Lilian Rushton raised a petition, the site was then registered with the Charity Commission and was thereby safeguarded against further inappropriate planning or development.